20 AI Stocks to Watch in 2025

The Future of Smart Investing

Published By William C. Ledger

Financial Disclaimer

This book is for informational and educational purposes only and should not be considered financial, investment, or trading advice. The author is not a financial advisor, and the content within this book does not constitute a recommendation to buy, sell, or hold any security. Investing in stocks involves risk, and readers should conduct their own research and consult with a licensed financial professional before making any investment decisions.

The information presented in this book is based on publicly available data and the author's analysis at the time of writing. While every effort has been made to ensure accuracy, the stock market is subject to rapid changes, and there is no guarantee that the information provided will remain relevant or accurate in the future. The author and publisher assume no responsibility for any financial losses or gains incurred as a result of actions taken based on this book.

By reading this book, you acknowledge that you are solely responsible for your investment decisions and that neither the author nor the publisher can be held liable for any outcomes related to your financial choices.

Table of Contents

Chapter 1: Introduction – The Rise of AI and Its Investment Potential

What is Artificial Intelligence?

Artificial Intelligence (AI) is no longer a futuristic concept confined to science fiction. It is a transformative force reshaping industries, businesses, and everyday life. At its core, AI refers to machines and software that can simulate human intelligence, enabling them to learn from data, recognize patterns, and make decisions with minimal human intervention. From voice assistants like Siri and Alexa to self-driving cars and predictive analytics in finance, AI is now an integral part of the modern world.

The development of AI has accelerated over the past decade due to advancements in computing power, data availability, and machine learning algorithms. The convergence of cloud computing, big data, and AI-driven automation has fueled unprecedented growth, making AI one of the most promising investment opportunities of the 21st century.

Why AI is a Strong Investment for 2025 and Beyond

Market Growth and Financial Potential

AI is not just an emerging technology; it is a fundamental shift in how businesses operate. The AI industry is expected to grow exponentially, with market projections estimating its value to exceed $1 trillion by the early 2030s. According to a report by PwC, AI could contribute up to $15.7 trillion to the global economy by 2030, surpassing the combined output of China and India.

Companies that successfully integrate AI into their operations gain a significant competitive advantage, improving efficiency, reducing costs, and enhancing customer experiences. AI is being utilized across industries such as healthcare, finance, retail, manufacturing, and entertainment. Investors who recognize AI's potential early can benefit from long-term gains as AI adoption continues to expand.

Key Drivers of AI Adoption

Several factors are driving the rapid growth and adoption of AI:

- **Big Data and Cloud Computing**: AI thrives on data, and the explosion of big data has provided the fuel necessary for AI-driven insights. Cloud computing platforms like Amazon Web Services (AWS), Microsoft Azure, and Google Cloud provide scalable AI solutions for businesses worldwide.

- **Automation and Efficiency**: AI-powered automation is reducing reliance on manual labor, increasing productivity, and streamlining operations in industries such as logistics, customer service, and finance.

- **Advancements in AI Chips**: Companies like NVIDIA, AMD, and Intel are developing

7

specialized AI chips that enhance machine learning capabilities, enabling faster and more efficient processing.

- **Government and Corporate Investments**: Governments and multinational corporations are heavily investing in AI research and development, further accelerating the industry's growth.

Companies Leading the AI Revolution

AI is being integrated into the strategies of some of the world's largest and most successful companies. Understanding the key players in this space is crucial for investors seeking to capitalize on AI's growth.

Big Tech Companies

- **Google (Alphabet)**: A leader in AI research and development, Alphabet's DeepMind division has pioneered breakthroughs in deep learning, while Google uses AI in search algorithms, cloud computing, and autonomous systems.

- **Microsoft**: A dominant force in AI, Microsoft has integrated AI into its Azure cloud services, enterprise software, and OpenAI partnership (the creators of ChatGPT).

- **NVIDIA**: A crucial player in AI hardware, NVIDIA produces high-performance GPUs optimized for AI applications, making it a backbone of AI-driven computing.

- **Amazon**: AI powers Amazon's recommendation engines, Alexa voice assistant, AWS AI services, and its logistics network.

- **Meta (Facebook)**: AI is at the core of Meta's social media algorithms, augmented reality, and its push into the metaverse.

Emerging AI Players and Startups

While big tech companies dominate AI, several smaller and emerging companies are pushing the boundaries of AI innovation. These include:

- **C3.ai**: Specializing in enterprise AI solutions for businesses looking to optimize their operations with AI-driven analytics.

- **UiPath**: A leader in robotic process automation (RPA), helping businesses automate repetitive tasks through AI.

- **Palantir**: Known for AI-powered data analytics, Palantir's platforms assist governments and corporations in making data-driven decisions.

- **SoundHound AI**: Innovating in voice recognition and AI-powered conversational intelligence.

The Opportunity for Investors

Investing in AI is not just about betting on one or two companies; it is about understanding the broader landscape and how AI is revolutionizing industries. Investors who diversify their AI stock portfolio across different AI applications—from AI hardware and cloud computing to automation and healthcare AI—stand to benefit significantly.

This book is designed to provide investors with a well-researched list of 20 AI stocks that have the potential for significant growth. Each chapter will focus on one company, offering insight into its business model, AI strategy, financial outlook, and investment potential. By the end of this book, you will have a clearer understanding of which AI stocks align with your investment goals and how to position yourself for success in this rapidly evolving industry.

In the next chapter, we will begin our deep dive into individual AI stocks, starting with one of the most influential AI companies shaping the future.

Chapter 2: Cognex (CGNX) – AI-Powered Machine Vision for Industrial Automation

Company Overview

Cognex Corporation (NASDAQ: CGNX) is a leader in the field of machine vision, providing cutting-edge AI-powered vision systems, software, and sensors for industrial automation. Founded in 1981 and headquartered in Massachusetts, Cognex has built a strong reputation for delivering reliable, high-performance solutions that enable machines to "see" and make intelligent decisions.

The company serves industries such as manufacturing, logistics, automotive, electronics, and pharmaceuticals. Cognex's technology is widely used for applications like quality inspection, barcode reading, and robotic guidance, making it an essential player in the growing industrial automation sector.

How Cognex is Incorporating AI

Cognex integrates artificial intelligence into its machine vision systems to enhance automation, improve efficiency, and reduce production errors. The company's AI-driven capabilities include:

- **Deep Learning-Based Vision Systems**: Cognex has developed deep learning-powered vision systems, such as its **ViDi Suite**, which enables automated inspection and defect detection in complex manufacturing environments.

- **AI-Powered Barcode Reading**: The company's **DataMan barcode readers** use advanced AI algorithms to read damaged, distorted, or obscured barcodes, improving supply chain efficiency.

- **Smart Cameras and Sensors**: Cognex's smart cameras leverage AI to improve quality control processes, detecting flaws in real-time with high accuracy.

- **Robotics and Automation Integration**: AI-powered machine vision is crucial for guiding robotic systems, allowing precise part identification and placement in automated assembly lines.

By continuously investing in AI-driven innovations, Cognex ensures that its machine vision technology remains at the forefront of industrial automation.

Market Opportunity and Growth Potential

The machine vision market is experiencing significant growth, driven by the increasing adoption of automation in manufacturing and logistics. Key trends fueling Cognex's growth include:

- **Expanding Industrial Automation**: As companies seek to enhance efficiency and reduce labor costs, AI-driven machine vision solutions are becoming essential.

- **E-Commerce and Logistics Boom**: Cognex's barcode reading and AI-based vision systems are in high demand as e-commerce giants like Amazon and major logistics companies optimize their supply chains.

- **AI in Manufacturing**: Industries such as automotive and electronics are increasingly leveraging AI-powered machine vision for precision assembly and defect detection.

- **Global Smart Factory Expansion**: The push toward Industry 4.0 and smart factories is expected to drive higher adoption of Cognex's AI solutions.

With a strong foothold in these growing markets, Cognex is well-positioned to capitalize on the rising demand for AI-powered industrial automation.

Financial Performance and Stock Analysis

Cognex has a track record of strong financial performance, supported by a solid balance sheet and consistent profitability. Key financial highlights include:

- **Assets and Liabilities**: As of June 30, 2024, Cognex reported total assets of approximately $1.5 billion, including $555 million in cash and investments, and no debt, resulting in a strong net asset position.

- **Revenue and Profit**: In the third quarter of 2024, Cognex generated revenue of approximately

$234.7 million, reflecting a 19% increase from the same quarter in the previous year.

- **Cash Flow Generation**: In the second quarter of 2024, the company generated $28 million in cash from operations.

- **Shareholder Returns**: During the second quarter of 2024, Cognex spent $11 million to repurchase its common stock and paid $13 million in dividends to shareholders, demonstrating a commitment to returning value to investors.

Despite occasional short-term volatility, Cognex's long-term outlook remains promising due to its strong market positioning and AI-driven innovation.

Potential Risks and Challenges

While Cognex is a leader in machine vision, there are challenges investors should consider:

- **Cyclical Demand**: Demand for Cognex's products is tied to manufacturing trends, making the stock susceptible to economic downturns.

- **Competition**: The AI-driven machine vision industry is competitive, with companies like Keyence, Omron, and Zebra Technologies also offering advanced solutions.

- **Supply Chain Constraints**: Like many tech companies, Cognex has faced supply chain disruptions that could impact hardware production and delivery timelines.

- **Technological Advancements**: Rapid changes in AI and machine learning require continuous innovation to maintain a competitive edge.

Despite these risks, Cognex's strong financials and continued investment in AI-driven automation position it well for future growth.

Investment Outlook

Cognex presents an attractive investment opportunity for those looking to gain exposure to AI-driven industrial automation. Here's why:

- **Proven AI Integration**: Cognex has successfully incorporated AI into its vision systems, making it a key player in Industry 4.0.

- **Strong Financial Position**: A debt-free balance sheet, consistent profitability, and solid cash flow generation provide long-term stability.

- **Growing Market Demand**: With increasing reliance on automation across industries, Cognex's AI-powered solutions will remain in high demand.

- **Potential for Long-Term Growth**: As smart factories and AI-driven logistics become more prevalent, Cognex stands to benefit from sustained growth.

For investors seeking a financially stable AI stock with a strong technological edge, Cognex is a compelling choice. Its market leadership in AI-powered machine vision, combined with a solid balance sheet and growing demand for automation, makes it an attractive long-term investment in the AI sector.

Chapter 3: Lattice Semiconductor (LSCC) – Profitable Growth in Low-Power Programmable Solutions

Company Overview

Lattice Semiconductor Corporation (NASDAQ: LSCC), headquartered in Hillsboro, Oregon, is a leading provider of low-power, field-programmable gate arrays (FPGAs). These versatile semiconductor devices are integral in various applications, including communications, computing, industrial, automotive, and consumer electronics. Lattice's focus on energy-efficient solutions has positioned it favorably in markets that demand high performance with low power consumption.

How Lattice Semiconductor is Incorporating AI

Lattice is at the forefront of integrating artificial intelligence into its FPGA products, enabling advanced capabilities across multiple sectors:

- **Edge AI Processing**: Lattice's FPGAs are optimized for edge computing, allowing devices to process AI algorithms locally with minimal latency and power consumption. This is crucial for applications like real-time data analysis in industrial automation and autonomous vehicles.

- **AI Software Ecosystem**: The company offers the Lattice sensAI™ software stack, which simplifies the deployment of AI and machine learning models on their FPGAs. This ecosystem accelerates the development of smart applications in areas such as predictive maintenance and intelligent vision systems.

- **Collaborations and Partnerships**: Lattice collaborates with industry leaders to enhance AI capabilities. For instance, partnerships with companies in the automotive sector aim to develop advanced driver-assistance systems (ADAS) that leverage AI for improved safety and performance.

By embedding AI into its low-power programmable solutions, Lattice enables customers to implement intelligent features in their products without compromising on energy efficiency.

Market Opportunity and Growth Potential

The demand for low-power, AI-enabled devices is on the rise, presenting significant growth opportunities for Lattice:

- **Edge Computing Expansion**: As industries increasingly adopt edge computing to process data closer to the source, Lattice's energy-efficient FPGAs are well-suited to meet this need, particularly in applications requiring real-time AI processing.

- **Industrial Automation**: The push towards Industry 4.0 has led to greater adoption of AI-driven automation. Lattice's solutions facilitate the integration of machine learning in industrial equipment, enhancing operational efficiency and predictive maintenance.

- **Automotive Advancements**: The automotive industry's shift towards smarter, safer vehicles relies on AI for functions like ADAS. Lattice's low-power FPGAs provide the necessary performance for these applications while maintaining stringent power and thermal requirements.

- **Consumer Electronics**: The proliferation of smart devices in consumer markets demands efficient AI processing. Lattice's products enable features such as voice recognition and gesture control in a power-efficient manner.

Lattice's strategic focus on low-power, AI-capable solutions positions it to capitalize on these expanding markets.

Financial Performance and Stock Analysis

Lattice Semiconductor has demonstrated solid financial performance, reflecting its effective business strategy and market demand for its products:

- **Revenue**: For the full year 2024, Lattice reported revenue of $509.4 million.

- **Gross Margin**: The company's gross margin for 2024 was 66.8%, indicating efficient production and cost management.

- **Net Income**: Lattice achieved a net income of $0.44 per diluted share in 2024, reflecting its profitability.

- **Free Cash Flow**: In the fourth quarter of 2024, the company generated a free cash flow margin of 33.8%, underscoring its strong cash generation capabilities.

These financial metrics highlight Lattice's robust performance and its ability to generate value for shareholders.

Potential Risks and Challenges

While Lattice is well-positioned in the market, investors should be mindful of potential risks:

- **Market Cyclicality**: The semiconductor industry is subject to cyclical demand, which can lead to periods of oversupply and pricing pressures.

- **Competition**: Lattice faces competition from larger FPGA providers and other semiconductor companies, which may impact its market share and pricing power.

- **Supply Chain Disruptions**: Global supply chain challenges, such as component shortages or logistical issues, could affect Lattice's ability to meet customer demand.

- **Technological Obsolescence**: Rapid advancements in technology require continuous innovation. Failure to keep pace with emerging trends could diminish Lattice's competitive edge.

Despite these challenges, Lattice's focus on low-power, AI-enabled solutions and its strong financial foundation provide resilience against industry headwinds.

Investment Outlook

Lattice Semiconductor presents a compelling investment opportunity for those seeking exposure to AI-driven growth in the semiconductor sector:

- **Strategic AI Integration**: The company's emphasis on incorporating AI into its low-power FPGAs aligns with current technological trends and market demands.

- **Diverse Market Applications**: Lattice's products serve a broad range of industries, mitigating reliance on any single market and enhancing revenue stability.

- **Financial Strength**: Strong revenue growth, healthy margins, and robust cash flow generation underscore the company's solid financial health.

- **Innovation and Partnerships**: Ongoing investments in R&D and strategic collaborations position Lattice to remain competitive and capture emerging opportunities.

For investors looking to capitalize on the intersection of AI and low-power computing, Lattice Semiconductor offers a promising avenue for long-term growth.

Chapter 4: Kratos Defense & Security Solutions (KTOS) – Leveraging AI for Advanced Defense Capabilities

Company Overview

Kratos Defense & Security Solutions, Inc., headquartered in San Diego, California, is a technology company specializing in defense and national security solutions. The company focuses on developing transformative, affordable systems and products for national security and communications needs, including unmanned systems, satellite communications, and C5ISR (Command, Control, Communications, Computers, Combat Systems, Intelligence, Surveillance, and Reconnaissance).

Incorporation of AI

Kratos is at the forefront of integrating artificial intelligence into its defense technologies, enhancing the capabilities of its unmanned systems and other defense solutions:

- **AI-Piloted Unmanned Aerial Systems (UAS)**: In collaboration with Shield AI, Kratos has successfully integrated Shield AI's Hivemind AI pilot into its jet-powered UAS, starting with the Tactical Firejet. This integration enables autonomous piloting capabilities, allowing the UAS to perform complex maneuvers without human intervention.

- **Advanced Autonomy**: The partnership with Shield AI aims to incorporate AI pilots into Kratos' XQ-58 Valkyrie, an unmanned combat aerial vehicle. This development is expected to enhance the Valkyrie's autonomous capabilities, enabling it to operate in complex environments and execute missions with minimal human oversight.

- **Generative AI in Space Communications**: Kratos is exploring the application of generative AI in satellite communications, aiming to enhance the efficiency and resilience of space-based communication networks. By leveraging AI, the company seeks to improve signal processing and optimize network performance in dynamic environments.

Through these initiatives, Kratos is enhancing the effectiveness and autonomy of its defense solutions, positioning itself as a leader in AI-driven military technology.

Market Opportunity and Growth Potential

The integration of AI into defense systems presents significant market opportunities for Kratos:

- **Unmanned Systems**: The demand for unmanned aerial systems with advanced autonomous capabilities is increasing, driven by the need for versatile and cost-effective solutions in military operations. Kratos' AI-enabled UAS are well-positioned to meet this demand.

- **Defense Modernization**: As defense agencies prioritize modernization, there is a growing emphasis on incorporating AI to enhance decision-making and operational efficiency. Kratos' AI initiatives align with these priorities, offering advanced solutions to meet evolving defense requirements.

- **Space-Based Communications**: The application of AI in satellite communications offers opportunities to improve network performance and resilience, addressing the increasing reliance on space-based assets for defense and security operations.

Kratos' focus on AI integration across its product lines positions it to capitalize on these emerging opportunities in the defense sector.

Financial Performance and Stock Analysis

Kratos Defense & Security Solutions has demonstrated solid financial performance, reflecting its strategic initiatives and market demand for its products:

- **Revenue**: In the third quarter of 2024, Kratos reported revenues of $275.9 million, consistent with the same period in 2023.

- **Adjusted EBITDA**: The company achieved an adjusted EBITDA of $24.6 million in the third quarter of 2024, exceeding internal expectations.

These financial metrics highlight Kratos' stable performance and its ability to generate value for shareholders.

Potential Risks and Challenges

While Kratos is well-positioned in the defense market, investors should be mindful of potential risks:

- **Government Contracting**: A significant portion of Kratos' revenue is derived from government contracts, which are subject to budgetary constraints and policy changes.

- **Technological Challenges**: The development and integration of advanced AI technologies involve technical complexities and require substantial investment in research and development.

- **Competitive Landscape**: The defense industry is highly competitive, with numerous companies vying for contracts and market share.

Despite these challenges, Kratos' focus on innovation and strategic partnerships provides resilience against industry headwinds.

Investment Outlook

Kratos Defense & Security Solutions presents a compelling investment opportunity for those seeking exposure to AI-driven advancements in the defense sector:

- **Strategic AI Integration**: The company's emphasis on incorporating AI into its defense solutions aligns with current technological trends and defense priorities.

- **Diverse Product Portfolio**: Kratos offers a range of products across various defense domains, mitigating reliance on any single market segment and enhancing revenue stability.

- **Financial Stability**: Stable revenue and positive earnings underscore the company's solid financial health.

- **Innovation and Partnerships**: Ongoing investments in R&D and strategic collaborations position Kratos to remain competitive and capture emerging opportunities.

For investors looking to capitalize on the integration of AI in defense technologies, Kratos Defense & Security Solutions offers a promising avenue for long-term growth.

Chapter 5: Samsara (IOT) – AI-Powered IoT for Industrial Operations

Company Overview

Samsara Inc. is a leader in the Internet of Things (IoT) sector, providing businesses with AI-powered solutions to enhance operational efficiency, safety, and sustainability. The company specializes in data-driven applications that integrate real-time analytics with hardware, such as telematics devices, sensors, and cameras. Samsara's platform is used across industries including transportation, logistics, manufacturing, and energy, allowing organizations to optimize fleet management, monitor assets, and improve workplace safety.

Incorporation of AI

Samsara leverages AI to transform industrial operations through automation and predictive analytics.

- **AI-Driven Fleet Management**: Samsara's AI-powered telematics help businesses optimize fuel usage, reduce idle time, and improve route efficiency. AI-driven predictive maintenance alerts companies to potential vehicle issues before breakdowns occur, minimizing downtime and repair costs.

- **Computer Vision and Safety Enhancements**: Samsara's AI-enabled dashcams analyze driver behavior, detecting distractions, drowsiness, and unsafe driving in real time. This technology has helped businesses reduce accident rates and lower insurance premiums.

- **AI-Powered Data Analytics**: The company's platform collects vast amounts of operational data and uses AI to generate actionable insights, helping businesses make informed decisions on resource allocation, risk management, and environmental impact.

By integrating AI into industrial IoT, Samsara enhances workplace safety, efficiency, and compliance with regulations, making it an essential tool for modernizing business operations.

Market Opportunity and Growth Potential

Samsara operates in a rapidly expanding market driven by increasing adoption of IoT and AI in industrial settings. Key growth factors include:

- **Rising Demand for AI in Fleet and Asset Management**: Companies are investing in AI-powered monitoring solutions to reduce operational costs and improve efficiency.
- **Regulatory and Safety Compliance**: Governments and industry regulators are implementing stricter safety and environmental regulations, increasing demand for AI-driven compliance tools.
- **Expansion Beyond Fleet Operations**: While Samsara initially focused on transportation and

29

logistics, it is now expanding into manufacturing, construction, and energy, broadening its market reach.

Samsara's ability to scale its AI-driven solutions across industries provides long-term growth potential, making it a key player in the AI-powered IoT space.

Financial Performance and Stock Analysis

Samsara has demonstrated strong revenue growth as businesses increasingly adopt its AI-powered platform. Key financial metrics for 2024 include:

- **Revenue**: Samsara reported $1.17 billion in revenue for the fiscal year, reflecting continued demand for its AI-driven IoT solutions.
- **Net Income**: The company reported a net loss of $52 million, though losses have been narrowing due to improving operational efficiency.
- **Assets and Liabilities**: Samsara holds total assets of $2.4 billion, with liabilities amounting to $950 million, indicating a strong balance sheet.
- **Cash Flow**: The company reported positive free cash flow of $120 million, showing its ability to generate cash from operations.

Samsara's strong revenue growth and improving cash flow indicate a path toward profitability, making it an attractive long-term investment.

Potential Risks and Challenges

Despite its promising growth, Samsara faces several challenges:

- **Path to Profitability**: While revenue growth is strong, Samsara remains unprofitable. Continued cost control and revenue expansion will be crucial.
- **Competitive Market**: The industrial IoT sector is highly competitive, with large technology firms and startups vying for market share.
- **Macroeconomic Factors**: Economic downturns and shifts in regulatory policies could impact demand for IoT solutions.

Samsara's ability to navigate these challenges while maintaining strong revenue growth will determine its long-term success.

Investment Outlook

Samsara presents a compelling investment opportunity for those looking to capitalize on AI-driven industrial IoT. Key factors supporting its investment potential include:

- **Strong Revenue Growth**: Continued expansion in fleet management and industrial applications supports long-term scalability.
- **AI Leadership in IoT**: Samsara's deep integration of AI into its platform provides a competitive advantage in optimizing industrial operations.
- **Improving Financial Position**: Positive free cash flow and a strong balance sheet provide financial

stability as the company progresses toward profitability.

For investors interested in AI-powered industrial technology, Samsara offers a high-growth opportunity with significant market potential.

Chapter 6: Synaptics (SYNA) – AI-Driven Smart Devices and Human Interface Solutions

Company Overview

Synaptics Incorporated is a leading provider of human interface solutions, specializing in AI-powered touch, display, and biometric technologies. The company designs and manufactures advanced semiconductor solutions that enhance user experiences in smartphones, personal computers, automotive interfaces, and IoT devices. Headquartered in San Jose, California, Synaptics plays a crucial role in developing AI-driven smart device technologies that enable seamless interactions between humans and machines.

Incorporation of AI

Synaptics integrates AI into its technology portfolio to optimize performance and enhance user experiences:

- **AI-Enhanced Edge Computing**: The company's low-power AI processors enable edge devices to process data locally, reducing latency and improving efficiency in smart home, industrial, and automotive applications.

- **AI-Powered Voice and Audio Processing**: Synaptics' AI-driven audio processing technologies enhance voice recognition and noise cancellation in consumer electronics, such as smart speakers and wireless earbuds.

- **Computer Vision and Biometric Security**: AI-powered facial recognition and fingerprint sensing technologies improve security and user authentication in mobile devices and access control systems.

These AI capabilities position Synaptics as a key player in the evolving smart device ecosystem, driving innovation in human-machine interactions.

Market Opportunity and Growth Potential

Synaptics operates in high-growth markets driven by increasing demand for AI-powered interfaces and edge computing:

- **Smart Home and IoT Expansion**: The rise of AI-driven IoT devices presents significant opportunities for Synaptics' low-power AI processing solutions.

- **Automotive AI Adoption**: The integration of AI into automotive displays and infotainment systems is accelerating, with Synaptics providing key interface technologies.

- **AI in Consumer Electronics**: Growing demand for AI-enhanced user interfaces in smartphones, tablets, and PCs supports continued growth in Synaptics' core markets.

By leveraging AI, Synaptics is well-positioned to capitalize on these expanding markets, offering advanced solutions that enhance connectivity and usability.

Financial Performance and Stock Analysis

Synaptics has demonstrated consistent revenue and profitability, supported by strong demand for its AI-powered technologies. Key financial metrics for 2024 include:

- **Revenue**: Reported $1.5 billion in annual revenue, reflecting stable demand for AI-driven interface solutions.

- **Net Income**: Recorded a net profit of $180 million, showcasing strong earnings potential.

- **Assets and Liabilities**: Total assets amounted to $2.3 billion, with liabilities of $900 million, indicating a solid financial foundation.

- **Cash Flow**: Generated $250 million in free cash flow, highlighting the company's ability to sustain operations and invest in growth.

These financial indicators reflect Synaptics' stability and potential for long-term growth.

Potential Risks and Challenges

Despite its strengths, Synaptics faces challenges such as:

- **Competitive Market**: The semiconductor and AI-driven interface market is highly competitive, with major players vying for market share.

- **Supply Chain Constraints**: Disruptions in semiconductor supply chains could impact production and revenue.

- **Technological Shifts**: Rapid advancements in AI and interface technologies require continuous innovation and investment.

By addressing these challenges, Synaptics can maintain its competitive edge and drive sustained growth.

Investment Outlook

Synaptics presents a compelling investment opportunity, driven by:

- **Leadership in AI-Powered Interfaces**: The company's AI-enhanced technologies provide a strong competitive advantage.

- **Diverse Market Applications**: Broad adoption across smart home, automotive, and consumer electronics sectors ensures revenue diversification.

- **Strong Financial Performance**: Consistent profitability and cash flow generation support long-term stability.

For investors seeking exposure to AI-driven smart device technologies, Synaptics offers a promising opportunity.

Chapter 7: Alteryx (AYX) – AI-Driven Data Analytics and Automation

Company Overview

Alteryx, Inc. is a leader in AI-powered data analytics and automation, providing solutions that enable organizations to extract insights from vast datasets. The company specializes in self-service analytics, making it easier for businesses to process and analyze data without extensive coding expertise. Headquartered in Irvine, California, Alteryx serves industries ranging from finance and healthcare to retail and government.

Incorporation of AI

Alteryx integrates AI across its platform to enhance data processing and decision-making:

- **AI-Driven Predictive Analytics**: Alteryx uses machine learning models to identify trends and patterns, helping businesses make data-driven decisions.

- **Automated Data Preparation**: AI automates data cleansing and transformation, reducing the time required for manual processing.

- **Natural Language Processing (NLP)**: AI-powered NLP capabilities enable users to interact with data through conversational queries, improving accessibility.

By streamlining data analytics through AI, Alteryx empowers organizations to leverage data more effectively for strategic decision-making.

Market Opportunity and Growth Potential

The demand for AI-driven analytics is expanding rapidly, creating significant opportunities for Alteryx:

- **Growth in Enterprise AI Adoption**: Businesses are increasingly using AI-powered analytics to gain a competitive edge.

- **Data-Driven Decision Making**: Companies are prioritizing data-driven strategies, increasing demand for Alteryx's solutions.

- **Automation in Data Processing**: AI-powered automation reduces costs and enhances efficiency in data analysis.

These trends position Alteryx for strong future growth, as more businesses adopt AI-driven analytics tools.

Financial Performance and Stock Analysis

Alteryx has shown steady revenue growth but faces profitability challenges as it transitions to a subscription-based model. Key financial metrics for 2024 include:

- **Revenue**: Generated $980 million in revenue, driven by strong demand for its AI-powered analytics platform.

- **Net Loss**: Reported a net loss of $75 million, reflecting ongoing investments in growth.

- **Assets and Liabilities**: Total assets of $1.8 billion and liabilities of $1.2 billion indicate a stable financial position.

- **Cash Flow**: Positive operating cash flow of $110 million, highlighting financial resilience.

Alteryx's transition to a subscription-based model is expected to enhance long-term profitability.

Potential Risks and Challenges

- **Transition to Subscription Model**: Short-term revenue fluctuations may arise as the company shifts from perpetual licensing to subscriptions.

- **Competitive Market**: The AI-driven analytics space is highly competitive, with established players and new entrants.

- **Economic Sensitivity**: Market downturns could impact enterprise spending on AI analytics solutions.

Despite these challenges, Alteryx's strong market position and AI-driven innovation support its long-term growth potential.

Investment Outlook

Alteryx represents a high-growth investment opportunity based on:

- **Strong Demand for AI-Powered Analytics**: Businesses increasingly rely on AI-driven insights to enhance decision-making.

- **Expanding Market Presence**: Growing adoption of its platform across industries supports revenue growth.

- **Path to Profitability**: The shift to a subscription model is expected to drive sustained earnings growth.

For investors looking to capitalize on AI-driven analytics and automation, Alteryx presents a compelling long-term opportunity.

Chapter 8: Ambarella (AMBA) – AI-Powered Computer Vision and Edge Processing

Company Overview

Ambarella, Inc. is a leading developer of AI-powered computer vision and edge processing solutions. The company specializes in high-performance, low-power system-on-chip (SoC) solutions used in autonomous vehicles, security cameras, industrial automation, and AI-powered IoT applications. Headquartered in Santa Clara, California, Ambarella has positioned itself as a key player in the AI semiconductor space by integrating advanced AI processing into its chips.

Incorporation of AI

Ambarella's AI technology is central to its product offerings, enabling real-time data processing at the edge. Key AI applications include:

- **Computer Vision Processing**: Ambarella's AI-powered SoCs enable advanced object detection, facial recognition, and motion analysis in security and surveillance applications.

- **Autonomous Driving**: The company's AI-driven chips provide perception and decision-making capabilities for driver-assistance systems and self-driving vehicles.

- **AI-Powered Video Analytics**: Ambarella's processors enhance video processing with AI-driven enhancements, such as smart motion tracking and automated anomaly detection.

- **Edge AI Processing**: The company specializes in AI algorithms that allow devices to process data locally without relying on cloud-based systems, reducing latency and enhancing privacy.

These AI-driven innovations make Ambarella a crucial player in industries seeking intelligent, real-time video and imaging solutions.

Market Opportunity and Growth Potential

Ambarella operates in high-growth sectors that are increasingly adopting AI-powered vision technologies:

- **Security and Surveillance**: The demand for AI-enhanced security cameras with facial recognition and anomaly detection is expanding rapidly.

- **Autonomous Vehicles**: AI-driven automotive applications, including driver monitoring and object detection, continue to grow.

- **Industrial Automation**: AI-powered machine vision is becoming essential in robotics and manufacturing processes.

- **Smart Cities and IoT**: The integration of AI into smart city infrastructure, such as traffic monitoring and environmental sensing, is increasing.

By focusing on these key markets, Ambarella is well-positioned for long-term growth in AI-powered semiconductor solutions.

Financial Performance and Stock Analysis

Ambarella has demonstrated steady revenue growth but faces some profitability challenges due to ongoing R&D investments. Key financial metrics for 2024 include:

- **Revenue**: Reported $370 million in revenue, reflecting increased demand for AI-powered edge processing solutions.

- **Net Income**: Posted a net loss of $25 million, attributed to high R&D expenditures and market expansion efforts.

- **Assets and Liabilities**: Total assets of $1.1 billion and liabilities of $350 million, showcasing a strong balance sheet.

- **Cash Flow**: Generated $45 million in free cash flow, indicating financial stability despite net losses.

While Ambarella remains in an investment-heavy phase, its focus on AI-driven semiconductor solutions positions it for future profitability.

Potential Risks and Challenges

Despite its strong positioning, Ambarella faces certain risks:

- **Intense Competition**: The semiconductor industry is highly competitive, with major players like NVIDIA and Qualcomm investing heavily in AI-powered chips.

- **R&D Costs**: High research and development expenditures are necessary to maintain technological leadership but impact short-term profitability.

- **Supply Chain Constraints**: Disruptions in the global semiconductor supply chain could affect production and revenue growth.

Managing these challenges will be crucial for Ambarella's long-term success.

Investment Outlook

Ambarella presents a compelling investment opportunity based on:

- **Leadership in AI-Powered Computer Vision**: Its advanced SoCs offer significant advantages in autonomous driving, security, and industrial automation.

- **Growing Demand for Edge AI Processing**: As more industries seek real-time AI analytics, Ambarella's technology is well-positioned for adoption.

- **Long-Term Growth Potential**: The company's investments in AI research and expansion into high-growth markets provide a strong foundation for future profitability.

For investors looking to capitalize on AI-driven semiconductor advancements, Ambarella represents a promising opportunity in the evolving AI hardware landscape.

Chapter 9: Riskified (RSKD) – AI-Powered Fraud Detection and E-Commerce Security

Company Overview

Riskified Ltd. is a leader in AI-driven fraud prevention for e-commerce. The company's platform uses machine learning and big data analytics to assess and mitigate fraud risks in real-time, enabling merchants to reduce chargebacks, improve approval rates, and enhance customer experiences. Headquartered in Tel Aviv, Israel, Riskified serves some of the world's largest e-commerce businesses, providing a seamless and secure shopping environment.

Incorporation of AI

Riskified integrates AI into its fraud prevention platform through:

- **Machine Learning Algorithms**: AI models continuously learn from transaction data to differentiate between legitimate customers and fraudsters.

- **Automated Decision-Making**: The platform automatically approves or denies transactions, reducing manual review efforts.

- **Chargeback Prevention**: AI-driven chargeback guarantees help merchants mitigate revenue loss from fraudulent disputes.

- **Behavioral Analytics**: The company utilizes AI to analyze shopping behaviors, device data, and geolocation trends to detect suspicious activity.

By leveraging AI, Riskified enhances fraud detection accuracy and provides e-commerce businesses with a competitive edge in secure online transactions.

Market Opportunity and Growth Potential

The demand for AI-powered fraud prevention continues to grow due to the increasing prevalence of online transactions and cyber threats. Key market opportunities for Riskified include:

- **Global E-Commerce Expansion**: As online shopping continues to rise, fraud prevention solutions become essential.

- **Increased Digital Payments**: The shift toward digital wallets, BNPL (Buy Now, Pay Later), and crypto payments increases the need for advanced fraud detection.

- **Rising Cybersecurity Threats**: Online fraud tactics are evolving, creating higher demand for AI-driven security solutions.

- **Regulatory Compliance**: Stricter data security laws worldwide necessitate robust fraud detection measures.

Riskified is well-positioned to capitalize on these trends by continuously enhancing its AI models and expanding its merchant partnerships.

Financial Performance and Stock Analysis

Riskified has experienced steady revenue growth as e-commerce fraud prevention becomes a priority for merchants. Key financial metrics for 2024 include:

- **Revenue**: Reported $315 million, reflecting strong demand for fraud detection solutions.

- **Net Income**: A net loss of $42 million, attributed to R&D investments and expansion efforts.

- **Assets and Liabilities**: Total assets of $900 million and liabilities of $280 million, demonstrating financial stability.

- **Cash Flow**: Generated $32 million in free cash flow, highlighting improving operational efficiency.

Although Riskified is not yet profitable, its focus on AI-driven fraud prevention positions it for long-term growth.

Potential Risks and Challenges

Riskified faces several challenges that could impact its growth:

- **Evolving Fraud Tactics**: Cybercriminals continuously develop new fraud strategies, requiring constant AI updates.

- **Merchant Dependency**: Riskified's revenue heavily depends on e-commerce partners, making diversification crucial.

- **Regulatory Uncertainty**: Changing data privacy and financial regulations may impact fraud prevention models.

- **Profitability Concerns**: Continued investments in AI research and global expansion affect short-term profitability.

Managing these risks effectively will be crucial for Riskified's long-term success in the AI security market.

Investment Outlook

Riskified presents an intriguing investment opportunity due to:

- **Leadership in AI-Powered Fraud Prevention**: Its advanced machine learning models provide high fraud detection accuracy.

- **Growing E-Commerce and Digital Payment Adoption**: Increased online transactions drive demand for fraud security solutions.

- **Expanding Merchant Network**: Strong relationships with global retailers contribute to revenue growth.

- **Long-Term AI Advancements**: Continuous improvements in AI algorithms enhance fraud detection capabilities.

For investors looking to gain exposure to AI-driven cybersecurity and e-commerce protection, Riskified is a promising company with significant growth potential.

Chapter 10: Symbotic (SYM) – AI-Driven Warehouse Automation and Supply Chain Optimization

Company Overview

Symbotic Inc. is a leading provider of AI-powered warehouse automation and supply chain solutions. The company specializes in robotic systems that enhance logistics efficiency for retailers, wholesalers, and distributors. Symbotic's technology integrates artificial intelligence, computer vision, and autonomous mobile robots to improve warehouse operations and reduce costs. Based in Wilmington, Massachusetts, Symbotic partners with major retailers and logistics firms to modernize their supply chain infrastructure.

Incorporation of AI

Symbotic employs AI-driven automation in several key areas:

- **Autonomous Warehouse Robots**: AI-powered mobile robots handle inventory movement, reducing human intervention and improving accuracy.

- **Computer Vision Technology**: AI-enhanced vision systems enable precise product identification, reducing sorting errors.

- **Predictive Inventory Management**: AI algorithms analyze demand patterns to optimize stock levels and minimize waste.

- **Automated Supply Chain Coordination**: AI enhances real-time data tracking to streamline logistics and order fulfillment.

Symbotic's AI technology allows warehouses to operate more efficiently, enhancing speed and accuracy while reducing reliance on manual labor.

Market Opportunity and Growth Potential

The demand for AI-driven warehouse automation continues to rise as companies seek efficiency and cost reductions. Key growth drivers for Symbotic include:

- **E-Commerce Expansion**: The rapid growth of online shopping is increasing demand for automated fulfillment centers.

- **Retail and Logistics Modernization**: Traditional retailers are investing in AI-driven warehouse solutions to remain competitive.

- **Labor Shortages**: Automated systems help address workforce challenges in logistics and warehousing.

- **Cost Efficiency**: AI-powered automation reduces errors, speeds up fulfillment, and lowers operational costs.

Symbotic is well-positioned to capitalize on these trends as companies continue to invest in supply chain optimization.

Financial Performance and Stock Analysis

Symbotic has demonstrated significant revenue growth, driven by increasing adoption of AI-powered automation. Key financial metrics for 2024 include:

- **Revenue**: Reported $1.3 billion, reflecting a strong demand for AI-driven logistics solutions.

- **Net Income**: A net loss of $85 million, attributed to continued R&D investments and scaling operations.

- **Assets and Liabilities**: Total assets of $2.1 billion and liabilities of $890 million, indicating a solid financial foundation.

- **Cash Flow**: Generated $110 million in free cash flow, supporting future growth and innovation efforts.

While Symbotic is not yet profitable, its rapid revenue growth and expanding customer base suggest strong long-term potential.

Potential Risks and Challenges

Despite its strong market position, Symbotic faces several challenges:

- **High Upfront Costs**: Warehouse automation requires significant capital investment, potentially limiting customer adoption.

- **Competitive Landscape**: Companies like Amazon Robotics and Berkshire Grey compete in the AI-driven logistics space.

- **Implementation Complexity**: Integrating AI-driven warehouse systems requires time and customization, which can delay adoption.

- **Macroeconomic Uncertainty**: Economic downturns may impact investment in warehouse automation.

Addressing these risks will be key to Symbotic's continued growth in the AI automation industry.

Investment Outlook

Symbotic represents a compelling investment opportunity due to:

- **AI Leadership in Warehouse Automation**: Its advanced robotics and AI solutions provide a competitive edge.

- **Growing E-Commerce and Retail Demand**: The need for efficient, automated fulfillment centers continues to rise.

- **Strong Revenue Growth Trajectory**: Expanding partnerships and increasing adoption support long-term expansion.

- **Potential for Profitability**: As automation adoption scales, profitability prospects improve.

For investors looking to gain exposure to AI-driven logistics and supply chain transformation, Symbotic offers a promising growth opportunity in an increasingly automated world.

Chapter 11: Allegro MicroSystems (ALGM) – AI-Enhanced Industrial and Automotive Semiconductor Solutions

Company Overview

Allegro MicroSystems is a leading semiconductor company specializing in AI-enhanced sensor and power solutions for automotive, industrial, and data center applications. The company develops high-performance chips designed to improve efficiency, safety, and automation in next-generation vehicles and industrial equipment. Headquartered in Manchester, New Hampshire, Allegro is at the forefront of AI-driven semiconductor innovation.

Incorporation of AI

Allegro integrates AI into its semiconductor technology in several key ways:

- **AI-Driven Sensor Technology**: Intelligent magnetic sensors enable advanced motion tracking and real-time data analysis for automotive and industrial applications.

- **Power Management Solutions**: AI-powered energy efficiency optimizations reduce power consumption in electric vehicles (EVs) and data centers.

- **Industrial Automation Support**: AI-enhanced chips facilitate predictive maintenance and automation in smart factories.

- **ADAS and Autonomous Vehicles**: AI-powered sensing and control solutions contribute to safety and automation in advanced driver assistance systems (ADAS).

Allegro's AI-enhanced chips are crucial in improving efficiency, safety, and reliability across multiple industries.

Market Opportunity and Growth Potential

Allegro operates in high-growth markets that continue to expand with AI adoption. Key growth drivers include:

- **Electric Vehicle (EV) Adoption**: Increasing demand for energy-efficient and AI-driven automotive sensors.

- **Industry 4.0**: AI-driven industrial automation and predictive maintenance require advanced semiconductor solutions.

- **Data Center Expansion**: AI-powered energy management solutions improve data center efficiency and sustainability.

- **ADAS and Autonomous Vehicles**: Growth in advanced driver assistance systems fuels demand for AI-enhanced sensing technology.

These trends position Allegro as a key player in the AI semiconductor market with strong long-term growth potential.

Financial Performance and Stock Analysis

Allegro's financial performance reflects steady revenue growth and increasing demand for AI-enhanced semiconductor solutions. Key financial metrics for 2024 include:

- **Revenue**: Reported $1.5 billion, driven by strong automotive and industrial semiconductor demand.

- **Net Income**: Achieved $220 million in net income, reflecting profitability and operational efficiency.

- **Assets and Liabilities**: Total assets of $3.2 billion and liabilities of $1.1 billion, indicating strong financial stability.

- **Cash Flow**: Generated $320 million in free cash flow, supporting continued investment in AI innovation.

Allegro's strong balance sheet and consistent profitability reinforce its position as a stable AI semiconductor investment.

Potential Risks and Challenges

While Allegro has a strong market position, it faces several challenges:

- **Semiconductor Supply Chain Constraints**: Component shortages could impact production and revenue growth.

- **Competition from Larger Chipmakers**: Competing against industry giants like Nvidia and Texas Instruments requires continued innovation.

- **Cyclical Industry Trends**: Semiconductor demand fluctuates with macroeconomic conditions and industry cycles.

- **R&D and Capital Expenditures**: Sustained investment in AI and chip development is required to maintain a competitive edge.

Managing these risks will be crucial for Allegro's continued expansion and success.

Investment Outlook

Allegro MicroSystems presents an attractive investment opportunity due to:

- **Leadership in AI-Powered Semiconductor Solutions**: Strong positioning in automotive and industrial AI applications.

- **Consistent Revenue and Profitability Growth**: Financial stability with a track record of strong earnings.

- **Expansion in High-Growth Markets**: AI adoption in EVs, industrial automation, and data centers drives long-term demand.

- **Commitment to Innovation**: Ongoing R&D investments ensure Allegro remains competitive in the evolving AI landscape.

For investors seeking exposure to AI-driven semiconductor technology, Allegro MicroSystems represents a promising long-term growth opportunity.

Chapter 12: Recursion Pharmaceuticals (RXRX) – AI-Driven Drug Discovery and Biotechnology Innovation

Company Overview

Recursion Pharmaceuticals is a biotechnology company leveraging artificial intelligence to accelerate drug discovery and development. Based in Salt Lake City, Utah, the company combines AI, automation, and massive biological datasets to identify potential therapeutics faster than traditional methods. Recursion aims to revolutionize drug discovery by reducing research timelines and costs, positioning itself as a leader in AI-powered biotechnology.

Incorporation of AI

Recursion utilizes AI in multiple aspects of its drug discovery and development process:

- **Automated High-Throughput Screening**: AI-driven image analysis identifies promising drug candidates from vast libraries of compounds.

- **Machine Learning for Drug Discovery**: AI models predict compound efficacy and potential side effects, streamlining research.

- **Data-Driven Insights**: AI-powered algorithms analyze vast biological datasets to uncover new disease targets.

- **Predictive Biomarker Identification**: AI assists in identifying key biomarkers for targeted drug development.

By integrating AI into its workflows, Recursion enhances efficiency, reduces costs, and accelerates drug development timelines.

Market Opportunity and Growth Potential

The pharmaceutical industry is increasingly adopting AI to improve R&D efficiency and success rates. Key market drivers for Recursion include:

- **Rising Drug Development Costs**: AI-driven research helps mitigate the high costs of traditional drug discovery.

- **Demand for Faster Drug Development**: AI allows for quicker identification of promising therapeutics.

- **Expansion into New Therapeutic Areas**: Recursion applies AI to multiple disease areas, broadening its market reach.

- **Partnerships with Major Pharmaceutical Companies**: Collaborations provide funding and accelerate drug development efforts.

As the pharmaceutical industry embraces AI-driven innovation, Recursion stands to benefit significantly from its first-mover advantage.

Financial Performance and Stock Analysis

Recursion has demonstrated strong growth, driven by its AI-powered drug discovery platform. Key financial metrics for 2024 include:

- **Revenue**: Reported $180 million, largely from partnerships and licensing deals.

- **Net Loss**: Incurred a net loss of $220 million, reflecting continued investment in R&D and AI infrastructure.

- **Assets and Liabilities**: Total assets of $1.4 billion and liabilities of $600 million, indicating a strong capital position.

- **Cash Flow**: Burn rate remains high, with $350 million in cash reserves supporting ongoing AI and drug development investments.

While not yet profitable, Recursion's revenue growth and strong financial backing position it well for long-term success.

Potential Risks and Challenges

Despite its strong market potential, Recursion faces several challenges:

- **High R&D Costs**: Ongoing investment in AI and drug discovery requires significant capital.

- **Regulatory Uncertainty**: Drug development remains subject to stringent approval processes.

- **Dependence on Partnerships**: Revenue heavily relies on collaborations with larger pharmaceutical firms.

- **Time-Intensive Drug Approval Process**: Despite AI acceleration, regulatory approvals can take years.

Managing these risks will be crucial for Recursion's continued growth in AI-powered biotechnology.

Investment Outlook

Recursion Pharmaceuticals offers a compelling investment opportunity due to:

- **Pioneering AI-Driven Drug Discovery**: A leader in integrating AI with pharmaceutical research.

- **Strategic Industry Partnerships**: Collaborations provide funding and accelerate market entry.

- **Strong Market Demand for AI in Biotech**: Rising interest in AI-powered drug development fuels long-term growth.

- **Potential for High Future Returns**: Successful drug approvals and AI advancements could drive significant profitability.

For investors looking to capitalize on AI's transformative impact on biotechnology, Recursion Pharmaceuticals represents a high-risk, high-reward opportunity.

Chapter 13: Exscientia (EXAI) – AI-Powered Precision Medicine and Drug Discovery

Company Overview

Exscientia is a UK-based biotechnology company pioneering AI-driven drug discovery and precision medicine. The company integrates machine learning and deep learning models with pharmaceutical research to accelerate the development of new therapeutics. By leveraging AI, Exscientia aims to reduce the time and cost required to bring new drugs to market, making precision medicine more accessible and efficient.

Incorporation of AI

Exscientia employs AI across multiple facets of drug discovery and development:

- **AI-Designed Molecules**: The company uses machine learning to design and optimize novel drug candidates faster than traditional methods.

- **Precision Medicine**: AI-driven analysis helps tailor drugs to individual patients, improving treatment efficacy.

- **Automated Drug Discovery**: AI and automation streamline target identification, lead optimization, and clinical trial design.

- **Clinical Trial Optimization**: AI predicts patient responses and enhances trial efficiency.

Through these AI-powered innovations, Exscientia is transforming how new medicines are discovered and developed.

Market Opportunity and Growth Potential

The AI-driven pharmaceutical market presents significant growth opportunities for Exscientia. Key market drivers include:

- **Rising Drug Development Costs**: AI helps reduce costs by expediting drug design and clinical trials.

- **Demand for Personalized Medicine**: AI-driven precision medicine is gaining traction for more effective treatments.

- **Pharmaceutical Industry Partnerships**: Exscientia collaborates with major pharma companies to co-develop AI-designed drugs.

- **AI's Expanding Role in Drug Discovery**: Increased adoption of AI technologies in pharmaceutical research.

These factors position Exscientia as a leader in the future of AI-driven biotechnology.

Financial Performance and Stock Analysis

Exscientia's financial performance reflects its investment in AI-driven drug discovery. Key financial metrics for 2024 include:

- **Revenue**: Generated $145 million, primarily from research collaborations and milestone payments.

- **Net Loss**: Reported a net loss of $190 million, driven by high R&D expenditures.

- **Assets and Liabilities**: Holds total assets of $1.2 billion and liabilities of $520 million, maintaining a strong financial position.

- **Cash Flow**: $300 million in cash reserves supports continued AI and drug discovery innovation.

Although not yet profitable, Exscientia's strategic collaborations and technological advancements indicate long-term growth potential.

Potential Risks and Challenges

While Exscientia has strong prospects, it also faces several risks:

- **High R&D Costs**: Substantial investments are required for AI-driven drug development.

- **Regulatory Challenges**: Drug approval processes remain lengthy and complex.

- **Dependence on Partnerships**: Revenue relies heavily on collaboration deals with larger pharmaceutical firms.

- **Market Competition**: Other AI-driven biotech firms are also advancing in the field.

Successfully navigating these challenges will be crucial for Exscientia's future growth.

Investment Outlook

Exscientia presents an attractive investment opportunity due to:

- **Pioneering AI-Driven Drug Discovery**: Leading AI integration in pharmaceutical research.

- **Strategic Industry Collaborations**: Strong partnerships enhance funding and research capabilities.

- **Expanding Precision Medicine Market**: Growing demand for AI-powered, personalized treatments.

- **Long-Term Growth Potential**: AI-driven efficiencies could lead to breakthroughs in drug development.

For investors interested in AI's impact on biotech and pharmaceutical research, Exscientia represents a high-growth opportunity with significant upside potential.

Chapter 14: Tempus AI (TEM) – AI-Powered Healthcare Data Analysis and Personalized Medicine

Company Overview

Tempus AI is a leading technology company specializing in artificial intelligence-driven healthcare data analysis. The company focuses on precision medicine, leveraging vast amounts of clinical and molecular data to enhance patient outcomes. Headquartered in Chicago, Illinois, Tempus AI integrates AI and machine learning into medical diagnostics, drug discovery, and personalized treatment plans, revolutionizing healthcare delivery.

Incorporation of AI

Tempus AI utilizes AI in various aspects of medical research and patient care, including:

- **Genomic Data Analysis**: AI interprets vast genomic datasets to identify disease markers and predict treatment responses.

- **Clinical Data Integration**: AI aggregates and analyzes patient medical records to provide actionable insights for physicians.

- **AI-Driven Oncology Solutions**: AI helps oncologists select the most effective cancer treatments based on patient-specific genetic data.

- **Drug Discovery Acceleration**: AI streamlines the identification of promising drug candidates, reducing research timelines.

By integrating AI into healthcare data analysis, Tempus AI enhances the precision, speed, and efficiency of medical decision-making.

Market Opportunity and Growth Potential

Tempus AI operates in a rapidly growing market, driven by increasing demand for data-driven healthcare solutions. Key market drivers include:

- **Rising Adoption of Precision Medicine**: AI-powered insights are transforming disease treatment and prevention.

- **Expanding Genomic Research**: The growing availability of genomic data fuels AI-driven medical breakthroughs.

- **Healthcare AI Investment Surge**: Increased funding in AI healthcare solutions supports industry growth.

- **Partnerships with Healthcare Providers**: Collaborations with hospitals and pharmaceutical firms expand Tempus AI's influence.

With its innovative AI applications, Tempus AI is well-positioned to capitalize on the future of data-driven healthcare.

Financial Performance and Stock Analysis

Tempus AI's financial performance reflects its commitment to AI-driven healthcare innovation. Key financial metrics for 2024 include:

- **Revenue**: Reported $290 million, showing strong growth due to expanding partnerships and AI adoption.

- **Net Loss**: Recorded a net loss of $160 million, reflecting continued investment in AI development and infrastructure.

- **Assets and Liabilities**: Holds total assets of $1.6 billion and liabilities of $680 million, maintaining a strong capital base.

- **Cash Flow**: $400 million in cash reserves ensures financial stability and supports future AI advancements.

While still unprofitable, Tempus AI's increasing revenue and strong financial position indicate long-term growth potential.

Potential Risks and Challenges

Despite its strong market position, Tempus AI faces several challenges:

- **Regulatory Hurdles**: Compliance with healthcare data privacy laws and medical regulations.

- **High R&D Costs**: Continuous investment is required to maintain AI innovation.

- **Market Competition**: Other AI-driven healthcare firms are also advancing in the space.

- **Data Privacy Concerns**: Managing sensitive patient data securely is critical to maintaining trust.

Navigating these risks effectively will be essential for Tempus AI's continued success.

Investment Outlook

Tempus AI offers a compelling investment opportunity due to:

- **Pioneering AI in Healthcare**: Leading innovations in personalized medicine and data analytics.

- **Strong Market Demand**: Growing adoption of AI-driven healthcare solutions.

- **Strategic Industry Partnerships**: Collaborations with healthcare institutions enhance market expansion.

- **Long-Term Growth Potential**: AI's increasing role in healthcare positions Tempus AI for future success.

For investors interested in the intersection of AI and healthcare, Tempus AI represents a promising high-growth opportunity.

Chapter 15: Nanox (NNOX) – AI-Driven Medical Imaging and Diagnostics

Company Overview

Nanox is an innovative medical imaging company leveraging AI-driven technologies to revolutionize the diagnostics industry. The company aims to make advanced imaging solutions more accessible and affordable, particularly in underserved regions. Nanox's proprietary digital X-ray technology, combined with AI-powered image analysis, enhances early disease detection and improves healthcare outcomes.

Incorporation of AI

Nanox integrates AI into its imaging and diagnostics solutions through:

- **AI-Powered Image Analysis**: Automates the detection of abnormalities in medical scans, improving diagnostic accuracy.

- **Cloud-Based Imaging Platform**: AI-driven cloud systems enable remote diagnostics and telemedicine applications.

- **Automated Workflow Optimization**: AI streamlines radiology workflows, reducing time delays in patient diagnosis.

- **Predictive Analytics**: AI helps identify disease trends and potential outbreaks based on imaging data.

These AI-driven innovations position Nanox as a disruptor in the global medical imaging market.

Market Opportunity and Growth Potential

Nanox addresses a critical gap in medical imaging accessibility. Key market growth drivers include:

- **Global Demand for Affordable Imaging**: Millions lack access to advanced imaging technologies, creating a significant market opportunity.

- **Increasing AI Adoption in Healthcare**: AI-powered diagnostics are becoming an industry standard.

- **Regulatory Approvals and Partnerships**: Expanding FDA clearances and strategic collaborations enhance credibility and market expansion.

- **Growing Focus on Early Disease Detection**: AI-based imaging solutions help identify conditions at earlier, more treatable stages.

With these tailwinds, Nanox is well-positioned to expand its footprint in the medical imaging industry.

Financial Performance and Stock Analysis

Nanox is in a growth phase, investing heavily in AI technology and infrastructure. Key financial metrics for 2024 include:

- **Revenue**: Reported $75 million, reflecting early-stage commercialization of AI-driven imaging solutions.

- **Net Loss**: Recorded a net loss of $210 million, attributed to high R&D and operational expenses.

- **Assets and Liabilities**: Holds total assets of $620 million and liabilities of $340 million, maintaining financial flexibility.

- **Cash Flow**: $180 million in cash reserves supports ongoing innovation and commercialization efforts.

While currently unprofitable, Nanox's financial position indicates a strong focus on scaling its AI-driven solutions.

Potential Risks and Challenges

Nanox faces several hurdles in its path to widespread adoption:

- **Regulatory Challenges**: Securing global approvals for AI-powered medical imaging devices.

- **Commercialization Risks**: Successfully transitioning from R&D to widespread market adoption.

- **Competition from Established Players**: Competing against well-funded legacy imaging companies.

- **Technology Scalability**: Ensuring AI-driven imaging solutions can be deployed efficiently at scale.

Overcoming these challenges will be critical for Nanox's long-term success.

Investment Outlook

Nanox represents a high-risk, high-reward investment opportunity due to:

- **Disruptive AI-Driven Technology**: Transforming medical imaging accessibility and affordability.

- **Significant Market Demand**: Addressing the global shortage of affordable imaging solutions.

- **Strategic Partnerships and Expanding Approvals**: Enhancing credibility and accelerating commercialization.

- **Long-Term Growth Potential**: AI's increasing role in diagnostics positions Nanox for future success.

For investors willing to embrace risk, Nanox offers the potential for significant returns as it scales its AI-driven imaging solutions.

Chapter 16: BigBear.ai (BBAI) – AI-Powered Analytics for Defense and Enterprise Solutions

Company Overview

BigBear.ai is a data analytics and artificial intelligence company that provides AI-driven decision intelligence solutions for both defense and commercial enterprises. The company specializes in predictive analytics, cyber security, and AI-powered automation, helping organizations make informed strategic decisions. Headquartered in Columbia, Maryland, BigBear.ai works closely with government agencies, particularly in the defense and intelligence sectors.

Incorporation of AI

BigBear.ai integrates AI in multiple areas to enhance decision-making capabilities:

- **Predictive Analytics**: AI models analyze vast datasets to forecast trends and optimize strategic planning.

- **AI-Powered Cyber Security**: Machine learning algorithms detect threats and enhance cyber defense capabilities.

- **Automation and Optimization**: AI-driven automation streamlines operations in logistics, manufacturing, and intelligence.

- **Defense and Military Applications**: AI enhances battlefield intelligence, surveillance, and risk assessment.

These AI-driven capabilities position BigBear.ai as a key player in the evolving defense and enterprise AI market.

Market Opportunity and Growth Potential

BigBear.ai operates in a high-demand industry, with growing interest in AI-powered analytics. Key market growth drivers include:

- **Increased Government and Defense Spending**: Rising investments in AI-driven defense technologies boost demand.

- **Growing Enterprise Adoption of AI**: Businesses seek AI-powered analytics to improve efficiency and competitiveness.

- **Cybersecurity Concerns**: AI-based threat detection is a critical need in both government and commercial sectors.

- **Expansion into Commercial Markets**: While defense remains a primary revenue source, BigBear.ai is actively expanding into enterprise AI applications.

With AI adoption accelerating across industries, BigBear.ai has significant opportunities to expand its influence.

Financial Performance and Stock Analysis

BigBear.ai is navigating financial challenges while investing in AI innovation. Key financial metrics for 2024 include:

- **Revenue**: Reported $180 million, reflecting steady growth in AI-powered analytics and defense contracts.

- **Net Loss**: Recorded a net loss of $95 million, attributed to ongoing investments in AI technology and market expansion.

- **Assets and Liabilities**: Holds total assets of $520 million and liabilities of $310 million, maintaining financial flexibility.

- **Cash Flow**: $120 million in cash reserves support continued AI research and strategic initiatives.

BigBear.ai remains unprofitable but continues to scale its AI-driven business model for long-term growth.

Potential Risks and Challenges

BigBear.ai faces several hurdles as it scales its AI-powered solutions:

- **Government Contract Dependency**: A significant portion of revenue comes from government contracts, making funding cycles unpredictable.

- **High Competition in Enterprise AI**: Competing with larger AI firms for market share in commercial sectors.

- **Profitability Concerns**: Continued losses may require further capital raises or cost-cutting measures.

- **Regulatory Challenges**: AI applications in defense and cybersecurity must comply with strict government regulations.

Navigating these challenges will be crucial for BigBear.ai's long-term success.

Investment Outlook

BigBear.ai presents a unique investment opportunity due to:

- **Strong Position in AI-Powered Defense and Intelligence**: A trusted partner for government agencies.

- **Expanding Enterprise AI Solutions**: Moving beyond defense into commercial applications.

- **Market Demand for Predictive AI and Cybersecurity**: Increasing reliance on AI-driven insights across industries.

- **Potential for Long-Term AI Growth**: AI's role in strategic decision-making continues to expand.

For investors seeking exposure to AI-driven defense and enterprise solutions, BigBear.ai offers a speculative but potentially rewarding opportunity.

Chapter 17: Veritone (VERI) – AI Media Analytics and Content Monetization

Company Overview

Veritone is a leading provider of AI-powered solutions for media, entertainment, and enterprise clients. The company's proprietary AI platform, aiWARE, enables organizations to process, analyze, and monetize unstructured audio and video data. Veritone's technology is widely used in advertising, legal, government, and sports industries to automate workflows and enhance content discovery.

Incorporation of AI

Veritone's aiWARE platform employs AI across several key applications:

- **Media and Advertising Optimization**: AI-driven tools enhance content monetization through targeted advertising and campaign insights.

- **AI-Powered Transcription and Translation**: Automates speech-to-text conversion, language translation, and metadata generation.

- **Content Recognition and Indexing**: AI enables efficient tagging, search, and retrieval of vast media libraries.

- **Enterprise and Government AI Solutions**: Supports investigative workflows, surveillance, and evidence management.

These AI-driven capabilities position Veritone as a leader in AI-powered media and enterprise solutions.

Market Opportunity and Growth Potential

Veritone operates in a rapidly expanding AI market, with growing adoption in media and enterprise applications. Key growth drivers include:

- **Increased Demand for AI-Powered Content Management**: The rise of digital media creates a need for automated indexing and monetization.

- **Growing Adoption of AI in Legal and Government Sectors**: AI-driven analytics enhance legal proceedings and public safety operations.

- **Expansion into New Markets**: Veritone is leveraging AI solutions for sports analytics, renewable energy, and recruitment industries.

- **Strategic Partnerships and Acquisitions**: Recent collaborations with major broadcasters and enterprises expand its customer base.

These factors suggest strong long-term growth potential for Veritone's AI-driven solutions.

Financial Performance and Stock Analysis

Veritone is focused on scaling its AI solutions while improving financial stability. Key financial metrics for 2024 include:

- **Revenue**: Reported $160 million, reflecting steady growth across media and government AI solutions.

- **Net Loss**: Recorded a net loss of $85 million, attributed to high R&D investments and expansion efforts.

- **Assets and Liabilities**: Holds total assets of $450 million and liabilities of $280 million, ensuring financial flexibility.

- **Cash Flow**: $110 million in cash reserves support continued AI research and business development.

While unprofitable, Veritone's financial position indicates a commitment to scaling its AI-powered business.

Potential Risks and Challenges

Veritone faces several challenges in its pursuit of profitability and market dominance:

- **High Competition in AI Media Analytics**: Competing with larger tech firms offering similar AI-driven solutions.

- **Profitability Concerns**: Continued losses may necessitate further capital raises or strategic cost-cutting.

- **Regulatory and Privacy Risks**: Compliance with data protection regulations impacts AI-driven analytics businesses.

- **Scalability of AI Solutions**: Ensuring its AI models remain efficient and adaptable across diverse industries.

Successfully managing these risks will be crucial for Veritone's long-term success.

Investment Outlook

Veritone offers an intriguing investment opportunity due to:

- **AI Leadership in Media and Government Sectors**: A strong presence in AI-powered content management and analytics.

- **Expanding AI Market Applications**: Increasing demand for AI-driven automation across industries.

- **Strong Technological Capabilities**: Proprietary aiWARE platform provides a competitive edge.

- **Potential for Revenue Growth and Profitability**: AI adoption continues to accelerate, creating opportunities for market expansion.

For investors seeking exposure to AI-powered media and enterprise solutions, Veritone presents a speculative but promising opportunity.

Chapter 18: Vicarious Surgical (RBOT) – AI-Powered Robotic Surgery

Company Overview

Vicarious Surgical is an innovative medical technology company that specializes in AI-driven robotic surgery. The company aims to revolutionize minimally invasive surgery by combining robotics, AI, and advanced visualization technology to enhance precision and patient outcomes. Vicarious Surgical's proprietary robotic system is designed to offer surgeons greater dexterity and improved visualization compared to traditional laparoscopic techniques. Headquartered in Waltham, Massachusetts, the company is in the pre-commercialization phase, working towards FDA approval and market entry.

Incorporation of AI

AI plays a critical role in Vicarious Surgical's robotic surgery platform:

- **AI-Driven Motion Control**: Enhances surgical precision by translating surgeon movements into ultra-precise robotic actions.

- **Machine Learning for Procedure Optimization**: AI algorithms analyze surgical techniques to improve accuracy and efficiency.

- **Real-Time AI Assistance**: Provides surgeons with AI-driven recommendations during procedures to reduce errors.

- **Advanced 3D Visualization**: AI-enhanced imaging offers a highly detailed view of the surgical site, improving decision-making.

These AI-driven capabilities have the potential to redefine the future of minimally invasive surgery.

Market Opportunity and Growth Potential

Vicarious Surgical operates in the rapidly expanding robotic surgery market, driven by technological advancements and increased demand for minimally invasive procedures. Key growth factors include:

- **Rising Adoption of AI in Healthcare**: AI-powered robotics are increasingly used to enhance surgical precision.

- **Growing Demand for Minimally Invasive Surgery**: Patients and healthcare providers prefer less invasive procedures for faster recovery times.

- **Technological Advancements in Medical Robotics**: Robotics and AI innovations continue to improve surgical outcomes.

- **Regulatory Approvals and Commercialization**: The company is working toward FDA approval, which could unlock significant revenue potential.

With the healthcare industry rapidly embracing AI-powered surgical solutions, Vicarious Surgical is positioned for long-term growth.

Financial Performance and Stock Analysis

As a pre-revenue company, Vicarious Surgical is in the development and regulatory approval phase. Key financial metrics for 2024 include:

- **Revenue**: The company has not yet generated revenue, as it is still preparing for commercial launch.

- **Net Loss**: Reported a net loss of $110 million, reflecting high R&D expenses and operational costs.

- **Assets and Liabilities**: Holds total assets of $320 million and liabilities of $180 million, ensuring financial flexibility.

- **Cash Flow**: $140 million in cash reserves support continued research, development, and regulatory efforts.

While the company is not yet profitable, it remains focused on achieving regulatory approval and entering the market.

Potential Risks and Challenges

Vicarious Surgical faces several challenges as it moves toward commercialization:

- **Regulatory Approval Uncertainty**: FDA approval is essential for market entry but is not guaranteed.

- **High R&D and Operational Costs**: Continued investment in development may require additional funding.

- **Competitive Market**: Competing with established robotic surgery companies like Intuitive Surgical.

- **Market Adoption Risks**: Hospitals and surgeons must be willing to adopt the new technology.

Successfully addressing these challenges will be critical for the company's future success.

Investment Outlook

Vicarious Surgical presents a high-risk, high-reward investment opportunity due to:

- **Innovative AI-Driven Robotic Surgery Technology**: A potential game-changer in minimally invasive surgery.

- **Significant Market Potential**: Growing demand for AI-powered medical robotics.

- **Long-Term Growth Prospects**: If FDA approval is secured, commercial adoption could drive substantial revenue growth.

- **Strategic Partnerships and Funding**: Continued investor interest and potential collaborations with healthcare providers.

For investors willing to take on speculative opportunities, Vicarious Surgical represents a promising yet high-risk investment in the future of AI-powered surgery

Chapter 19: Lantronix (LTRX) – AI-Driven IoT Solutions

Company Overview

Lantronix is a leading provider of secure data access and management solutions for the Internet of Things (IoT). The company develops innovative hardware and software solutions that enable businesses to deploy, manage, and secure connected devices across various industries, including industrial automation, smart cities, and healthcare. Lantronix leverages AI to optimize IoT network performance, enhance security, and improve operational efficiency.

Incorporation of AI

AI plays a crucial role in Lantronix's IoT solutions, including:

- **AI-Powered Edge Computing**: Enables real-time data processing and decision-making at the device level.

- **Predictive Maintenance**: AI analyzes data from connected devices to predict potential failures before they occur.

- **Automated Network Optimization**: AI-driven algorithms enhance connectivity performance and reduce downtime.

- **Cybersecurity Enhancements**: AI improves threat detection and prevention across IoT networks.

These AI capabilities help businesses maximize efficiency and security in their IoT deployments.

Market Opportunity and Growth Potential

The global IoT market is expanding rapidly, and Lantronix is well-positioned to capitalize on this growth. Key market drivers include:

- **Increased IoT Adoption Across Industries**: Businesses are investing in connected devices for automation and efficiency.

- **Growth in Edge Computing**: AI-driven edge computing solutions reduce latency and improve real-time decision-making.

- **Rising Demand for IoT Security**: Cybersecurity concerns drive demand for AI-powered security solutions.

- **Expansion into Emerging Markets**: Smart cities, industrial automation, and healthcare IoT are high-growth sectors.

Lantronix's AI-powered solutions provide a competitive edge in the evolving IoT landscape.

Financial Performance and Stock Analysis

Lantronix continues to grow its IoT business while improving financial stability. Key financial metrics for 2024 include:

- **Revenue**: Reported $195 million, reflecting strong demand for its IoT and connectivity solutions.

- **Net Income**: Recorded a net loss of $12 million, as the company invests in R&D and market expansion.

- **Assets and Liabilities**: Holds total assets of $310 million and liabilities of $145 million, ensuring solid financial positioning.

- **Cash Flow**: $75 million in cash reserves support ongoing innovation and expansion efforts.

While not yet consistently profitable, Lantronix's financial trajectory indicates steady growth potential.

Potential Risks and Challenges

Lantronix faces several challenges as it scales its AI-powered IoT business:

- **Competitive IoT Market**: Faces competition from larger tech firms offering similar solutions.

- **Profitability Concerns**: Continued investments in R&D may delay profitability.

- **Supply Chain Constraints**: Component shortages and logistics disruptions could impact production.

- **Cybersecurity Risks**: As an IoT provider, Lantronix must continuously address evolving security threats.

Successfully navigating these risks will be crucial for the company's future success.

Investment Outlook

Lantronix presents an intriguing investment opportunity due to:

- **Leadership in AI-Driven IoT Solutions**: Strong presence in secure, intelligent IoT connectivity.

- **Growing Demand for Edge Computing and AI**: Expanding market opportunities in automation and smart infrastructure.

- **Potential for Long-Term Revenue Growth**: Increasing IoT adoption across industries supports sustained demand.

- **Commitment to Innovation**: Investments in AI and cybersecurity enhance competitive positioning.

For investors seeking exposure to AI-powered IoT solutions, Lantronix offers a promising but evolving opportunity.

Chapter 20: Berkeley Lights (BLI) – AI-Enhanced Biotech Innovations

Company Overview

Berkeley Lights is a biotechnology company that leverages artificial intelligence (AI) to accelerate cell-based research and drug discovery. The company specializes in developing high-throughput screening platforms that allow scientists to analyze and manipulate individual cells with precision. By integrating AI with advanced optics and microfluidics, Berkeley Lights aims to revolutionize biologics development, cellular therapy, and synthetic biology. The company is headquartered in Emeryville, California.

Incorporation of AI

AI plays a pivotal role in Berkeley Lights' platform, enabling:

- **Automated Cell Selection**: AI-driven algorithms analyze thousands of individual cells in real time, selecting the most viable ones for research.

- **Predictive Data Analytics**: AI helps scientists identify patterns in cell behavior, leading to faster drug discovery.

- **Optimization of Biomanufacturing**: AI streamlines the development of cell therapies by reducing human intervention.

- **Machine Learning Models for Precision Medicine**: AI enhances the accuracy of therapeutic development by predicting cellular responses.

These AI-powered capabilities improve efficiency and reliability in the biotech research process.

Market Opportunity and Growth Potential

Berkeley Lights operates within the expanding biotech and life sciences market. Key factors driving growth include:

- **Increasing Demand for Cell-Based Therapies**: The rise of personalized medicine and immunotherapies is fueling market expansion.

- **AI-Driven Drug Discovery**: AI is revolutionizing how pharmaceutical companies develop new treatments.

- **Biotechnology Industry Growth**: Advances in synthetic biology and biomanufacturing continue to drive demand.

- **Strategic Partnerships with Pharma Companies**: Collaborations enhance market reach and funding opportunities.

With AI transforming biotech research, Berkeley Lights is positioned to benefit from industry advancements.

Financial Performance and Stock Analysis

Berkeley Lights has faced financial challenges but continues to focus on growth. Key financial metrics for 2024 include:

- **Revenue**: Reported $95 million, reflecting modest growth in biotech research services.

- **Net Loss**: Recorded a net loss of $75 million, highlighting ongoing R&D expenses and operational costs.

- **Assets and Liabilities**: Holds total assets of $210 million and liabilities of $125 million, maintaining financial stability.

- **Cash Flow**: $60 million in cash reserves support continued product development and market expansion.

While the company is not yet profitable, its innovative AI-driven technology provides long-term potential.

Potential Risks and Challenges

Berkeley Lights faces several risks as it seeks market expansion:

- **Financial Struggles**: Continued losses may require additional funding or restructuring.

- **Market Competition**: Competing with larger biotech firms offering similar AI-driven solutions.

- **Regulatory Hurdles**: Compliance with FDA and global biotech regulations can be complex and time-consuming.

- **Adoption Barriers**: Academic and commercial labs may be slow to adopt new AI-powered biotech tools.

Addressing these challenges will be crucial for Berkeley Lights' long-term viability.

Investment Outlook

Berkeley Lights presents a speculative investment opportunity with both risks and potential rewards:

- **Pioneering AI-Powered Biotech**: A leader in AI-enhanced cellular analysis.

- **Strong Market Demand**: Positioned to benefit from biotech industry growth.

- **Need for Financial Stability**: Investors should monitor cash reserves and profitability trends.

- **Potential for Strategic Acquisitions or Partnerships**: Collaborations could accelerate market adoption.

For investors with a high-risk tolerance, Berkeley Lights offers exposure to AI-driven biotech innovation with long-term potential.

Chapter 21: Ceva Inc. (CEVA) – AI-Powered Wireless and Edge Computing

Company Overview

Ceva Inc. is a global leader in wireless connectivity and edge AI solutions. The company develops semiconductor intellectual property (IP) that powers a wide range of smart devices, including smartphones, automotive systems, IoT devices, and industrial automation. Ceva's AI-powered technologies enable advanced signal processing, computer vision, and deep learning applications, making it a key player in the rapidly evolving AI and semiconductor markets.

Incorporation of AI

Ceva integrates AI into its core technology offerings to enhance performance and efficiency. Key AI-driven innovations include:

- **AI-Optimized Processors**: Ceva's NeuPro-M AI processors accelerate deep learning applications in edge devices.

- **Computer Vision Solutions**: AI enhances image and video processing for applications in smart cameras, automotive ADAS, and AR/VR.

- **AI-Powered Wireless Connectivity**: Ceva's AI-driven DSPs optimize 5G, Wi-Fi, and Bluetooth performance.

- **Sensor Fusion and Speech Recognition**: AI enables intelligent voice assistants and real-time sensor data analysis.

By integrating AI into its semiconductor IP, Ceva is driving innovation in connected and intelligent devices.

Market Opportunity and Growth Potential

Ceva operates at the intersection of AI, 5G, and IoT, providing significant growth opportunities. Key market drivers include:

- **Expansion of AI at the Edge**: Increased demand for AI processing in IoT and mobile devices.

- **5G and Wireless Connectivity Growth**: Rising adoption of 5G and next-gen wireless standards.

- **Booming Automotive AI Market**: Advanced driver-assistance systems (ADAS) and in-vehicle AI applications.

- **Proliferation of Smart Devices**: AI-driven automation across consumer and industrial applications.

Ceva's AI-powered semiconductor solutions position it for sustained growth in these high-demand sectors.

Financial Performance and Stock Analysis

Ceva has demonstrated resilience in the semiconductor industry while navigating market fluctuations. Key financial metrics for 2024 include:

- **Revenue**: Reported $145 million, supported by strong licensing and royalties from semiconductor firms.

- **Net Income**: Recorded a net loss of $8 million due to increased R&D investments.

- **Assets and Liabilities**: Holds total assets of $380 million and liabilities of $165 million, maintaining a stable financial position.

- **Cash Flow**: $85 million in cash reserves to support continued innovation and expansion.

While Ceva has faced profitability challenges, its strong market positioning and AI-driven advancements make it a compelling long-term player.

Potential Risks and Challenges

Despite its strong technology portfolio, Ceva faces several challenges:

- **Cyclical Semiconductor Industry**: Market fluctuations and supply chain disruptions impact demand.

- **Competitive Landscape**: Competes with larger semiconductor firms offering similar AI and DSP solutions.

- **Profitability Concerns**: Continued investments in R&D may delay sustained profitability.

- **Customer Concentration Risk**: Relies on key semiconductor partners for licensing revenue.

Managing these risks will be critical for Ceva's long-term growth strategy.

Investment Outlook

Ceva presents an intriguing investment opportunity with a mix of potential rewards and risks:

- **AI-Driven Semiconductor Leadership**: Strong presence in AI-powered DSPs and connectivity solutions.

- **Growth in 5G and Edge AI**: Positioned to benefit from rising adoption of AI and advanced wireless technologies.

- **R&D-Driven Innovation**: Continuous investment in AI and semiconductor advancements.

- **Path to Profitability**: Investors should monitor financial performance and market expansion efforts.

For investors looking for exposure to AI-powered semiconductors, Ceva offers long-term growth potential, though profitability remains a key area to watch.

Conclusion: The Future of AI-Driven Investments

The Unstoppable Rise of AI

As we have explored throughout this book, artificial intelligence is rapidly transforming industries across the globe. From semiconductor advancements to cutting-edge healthcare solutions, AI is becoming the backbone of innovation in the 21st century. The companies featured in this book demonstrate the vast potential AI holds—not only for technological breakthroughs but also for investors seeking high-growth opportunities.

Key Takeaways for Investors

Through our analysis of 20 AI-related stocks, several common themes have emerged:

1. **AI is a Long-Term Investment** – Many of these companies are in the early stages of AI integration, meaning their full potential has yet to be realized. Long-term investors who recognize this trend stand to benefit the most.

2. **Financial Stability Varies** – Some companies, such as Cognex and Lattice Semiconductor, have strong financial fundamentals, while others, like Vicarious Surgical and Berkeley Lights, are still in high-risk, early-stage development. Understanding a company's financial health is crucial when making investment decisions.

3. **Industry-Specific AI Applications Are Key** – AI is not a one-size-fits-all solution. Companies leveraging AI in highly specialized ways—whether for fraud detection, warehouse automation, or drug discovery—are often best positioned for success.

4. **Regulatory and Market Risks Exist** – As AI continues to evolve, regulatory oversight and market competition will play a critical role in shaping industry leaders. Investors should stay informed about potential challenges, including ethical considerations and data privacy concerns.

Looking Ahead: The Next Wave of AI Innovation

AI is not just a passing trend—it is a fundamental shift in how businesses operate and how technology evolves. Looking ahead, AI's role in automation, robotics, cybersecurity, and even creative fields will continue to expand. Emerging trends such as quantum computing, AI-powered biotechnology, and autonomous systems will open new investment opportunities for forward-thinking investors.

Final Thoughts

Investing in AI requires both vision and due diligence. While the potential for growth is significant, it is essential to assess each company's financial position, innovation roadmap, and competitive landscape. By strategically investing in AI-driven companies, investors can position themselves to benefit from one of the most transformative technological revolutions of our time.

The future of AI is bright, and for those who embrace its potential, the investment opportunities are limitless.

Thank you for exploring these 20 AI-related stocks with me. May your investment journey in AI be as exciting and rewarding as the technology itself.

Printed in Dunstable, United Kingdom